drew

Rembrandt's surrealist period:
'Self portrait on the night of the long knaves"

Camp David
Nonsense in Art

the rake of the sabine women

...and here's one I painted earlier.

Camp David
Nonsense in Art

Drawings and Verses
by
Simon Drew

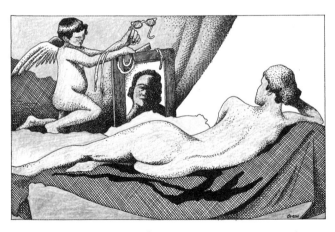

Why! Miss Jones! You're beautiful!

ANTIQUE COLLECTORS CLUB

to Caroline
and to all
the dartmouth artists

© 1992 Simon Drew
World copyright reserved

ISBN 1 85149 162 7

British Library Cataloguing in Publication Data
Drew, Simon
Camp David: Nonsense in Art
I. Title
709

Published and printed in England by the Antique Collectors' Club Ltd.
Woodbridge, Suffolk

MOLE FLANDERS

Frans Hals' first attempts :

the
laughing
proboscis
monkey

the
laughing
chandelier

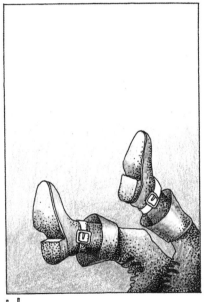

the
hysterical
cavalier

drew

the
laughing
cavalier
(having laughed
his head off)

drew

The critic proclaimed with a cough
that the painting was not by Van Gogh,
and he said as he sipped at his hock:
I'm sure that it isn't Van Gogh,
and the tartan rug spread by the loch
is not in the style of Van Gogh.
It also may please you to know
it is certainly not by Van Gogh".

el gecko and anonymous bosch

a portrait for the future:

Lenny's Drawer

Mrs da Vinci was always annoyed
Lenny, her son, would confess
that though he had faults he tried to avoid,
his bedroom was always a mess.

"Look at this drawer; it's a crying disgrace;
rubbish from goodness knows when.
And how did you get all that paint on
your face?
Has Lisa been playing again?

You dream up contraptions like
submarine toys,
but never a knife to cut bread.
Why can't you be like the other young boys?
Invent something useful instead."

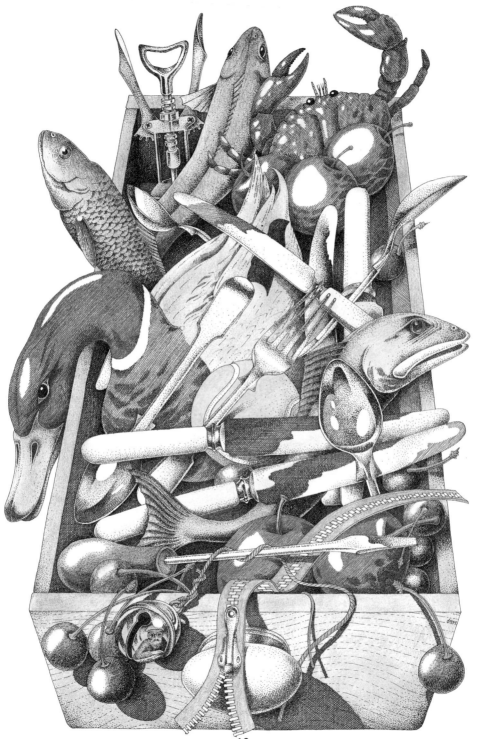

13

some day my plinth will come

sickert as a parrot

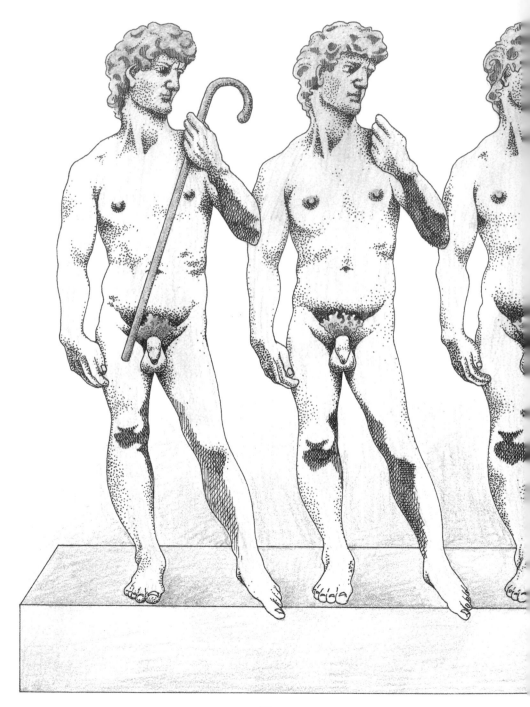

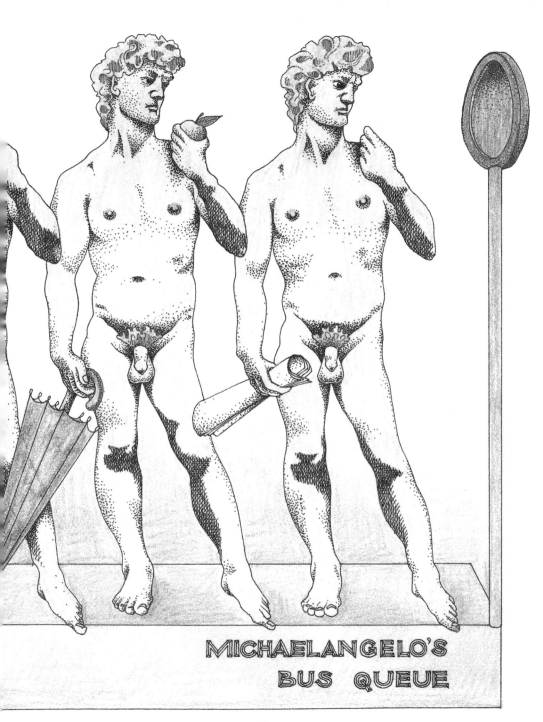

MICHAELANGELO'S
BUS QUEUE

It's November the 12th:
he's in one of his baths
and old Uncle Wilf's growing weaker.
You know how in life
you've the choice of two paths:
it's rubber duck death or Eureka.

(so send your wreaths to me please
as he's no Archimedes).

A Ballad   (to be sung in a
             country and western style)

Van Gogh died at 90
in a motel near L.A.
Most folk think he shot himself
in places far away.
But if you hear my story
and want to know the truth
a man from Mississippi
saw the talent in this youth.
He made him sign a contract
and Vincent didn't care:
he signed it in vermilion
and even made a spare.
Then he fetched a handgun
and faked the suicide;
later all the galleries
would think that he had died.
Back in Mississippi
his friend began to deal
selling all the paintings
for a price that wasn't real.
Vincent now was happy
for he got half the cash
even though his masterpieces
went to men so brash.
Ask him how he spent the dough,
you couldn't make him speak;
mention sunflowers to him —
he'd laugh for half a week.

21

"On discovering that
the paintings in an exhibition
were wrongly labelled."

Most visitors seemed overjoyed
but the critic I heard was annoyed:
'The hanging committee
deserves all my pity,
for instance this Bacon is Freud.'

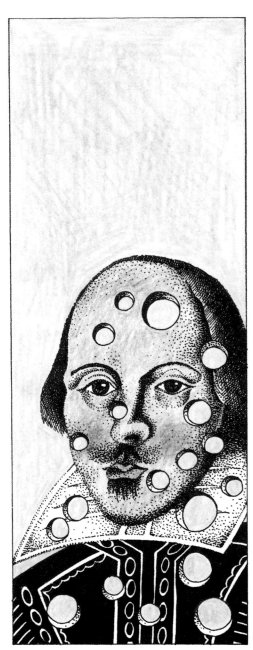

shakespeare
with holes

no holes bard

23

poultry in motion

25

mollusc of the glen

'Of course, the sign of a really good painting is when they follow you round the room.'

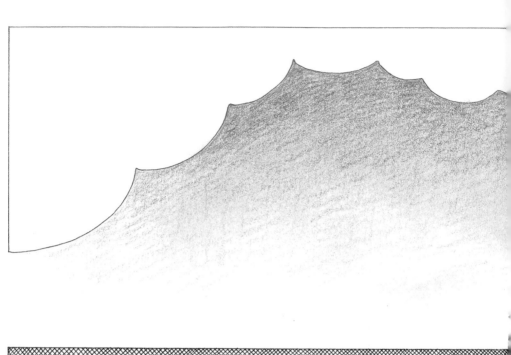

st. francis talking at crossed porpoises

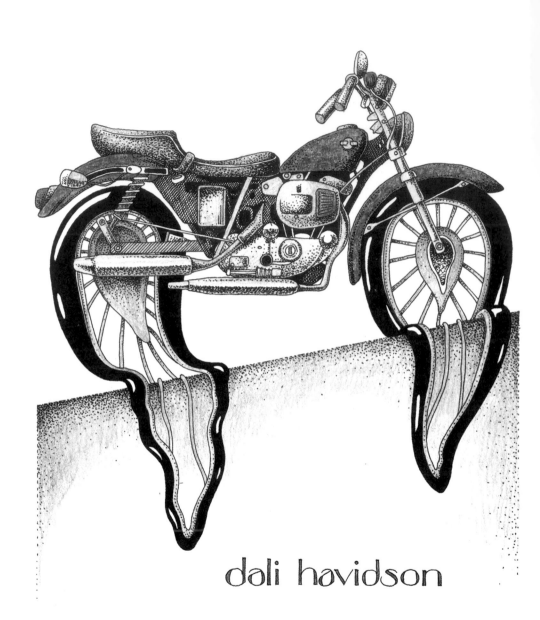

dali havidson

Le Déjeuner sur l'Herbe

(Manet!
  O Manet!
  I'd walk a million miles
  for one of your smiles
  O Manet!)

Now, this is how
you fit a
contact lens

If I couldn't do this
I wanted to be
a traindriver

So, as usual: it's
two submissions
or a knockout

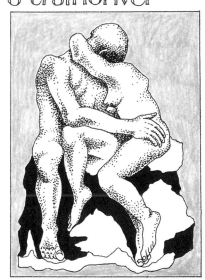

so this is
reflexology,
is it?

What happened to
your last husband,
Mrs. Rodin ?

Yes, Mrs. Arbuthnot,
you need two
fillings

My mother always said
if the wind changed we'd
be stuck like this

I'm not sure if there
is an antidote
to superglue

Ode to J.M.W. Turner

Turner was a hooligan,
a fact that's little known:
he drank too much on Friday nights
and wore a traffic cone.

His watercolours throbbed with life;
his vivid sunsets burst.
But every week on Friday nights
he thought of lager first.

He painted ships on weekdays
or gentle waterfalls
but when it came to Friday nights
he wrote on toilet walls.

rejected headlines:

"Salvador Dali's moustache was a fake."
"Monet could only paint moles."
"Renoir once leapt with no clothes
                              from a cake."
"Toulouse-Lautrec stood in holes."

Botticelli's Candy Floss Seller

(When you're down on the beach in Lyme Regis
reminding yourself of the smell,
the first thing you see is a kiosk
with a naked girl stood in a shell.)

How many
mince pies
so far, Caesor?   ...et tu, Brute.

'...frankly, my dear, I don't give Adam.'

When David met Venus de Milo
it seemed such a harmless affair
but the offspring were little fat cherubs
that had to be put into care.
And when these grew older and virile
they fathered some more of their own;

(which is all really rather surprising
when you realise they're made out of stone

and in different countries).

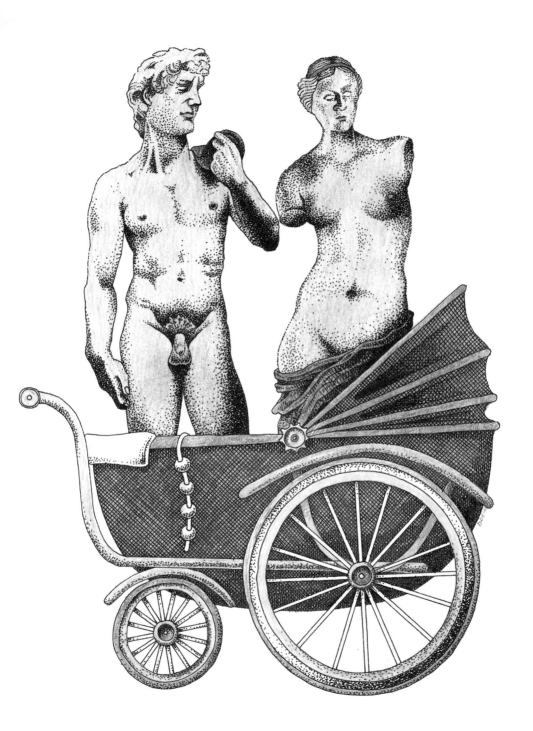

hares and graces

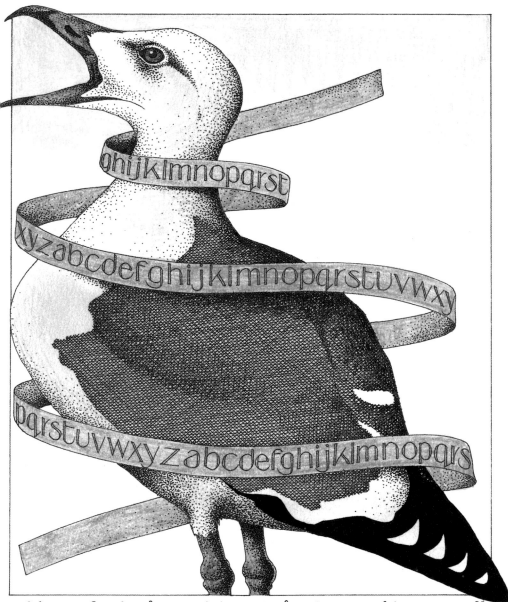

a friend of mine's a critic who's changed into a gull,
and though his life is brighter, his writing now seems dull;
for while his methods altered, he never lost his flair:
what he did on paper, he now does from the air.   drew

A Mystery Solved

It seemed that all Europe was asking.
The tongues in the cafés would wag:
Why does he nibble a goldfish?
What does he keep in the bag?

Degas was not a surrealist
(he's never been given that tag).
So why did he nibble a goldfish?
What did he keep in that bag?

Sometimes he'd paint ballerinas
and never chose young men in drag.
So why did he nibble a goldfish?
What did he keep in the bag?

But when he was painting for hours
and, feeling his energy flag,
he'd have a quick bite at a goldfish
which (of course) he had kept in the bag.

' Time for bed, Pablo. '

Gainsborough's surrealist period:
"The Blue Boy in Squid Row."